*To Todd, for laughing with me after the crazy happens, especially if I can't laugh in the moment.
We do have good stories to tell.
And to my dad. The turning-down-the-volume page is especially for you. I get it now.*

Father's Day Shapes
By Lindsey Michaels

Copyright © 2024 by Lindsey Michaels
ISBN 979-8-9881864-3-4

All rights reserved. No portion of this book may be used or reproduced in any matter whatsoever without written permission from the publisher. For permissions contact: Lmichaelsbooks@gmail.com

FATHER'S DAY
SHAPES

LINDSEY MICHAELS

This is a circle.

But on Father's Day, this shape is called *protection*.

Dads step in and protect kids when their best ideas with circles are not actually the best ideas.

This is a triangle.

But on Father's Day, this shape is called *volume*.

This is because when Dad tells his kids something and they don't listen, he has to say it louder.

When a triangle is turned this way, it's still a triangle.

But on Father's Day,
this shape is called *begging*.

It's for when Dad asks nicely and then begs his kids to please, please, please, be a little quieter.

Please.

Please.

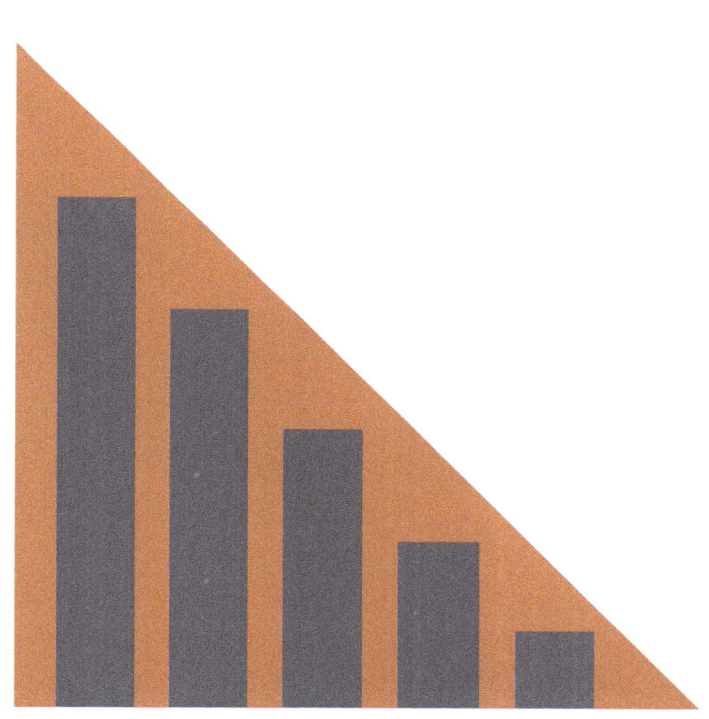

This is a semicircle.

But on Father's Day, this shape is called *jokes*.

Dad jokes, that is.
Dad jokes that are normally not funny are completely funny on Father's Day.
Everyone will laugh hysterically.
Go ahead and try it, you'll see.

This is a star.

But on Father's Day, this shape is called *the 5 senses*.

When Dad became a dad,

he smelled things
he'd never smelled before.
He saw messes
like he'd never seen before.
He heard crying
like he'd never heard before.
He stepped on things
he'd never stepped on before.
He ate in ways
he'd never eaten before.

(It's okay. It's all for a very good cause.)

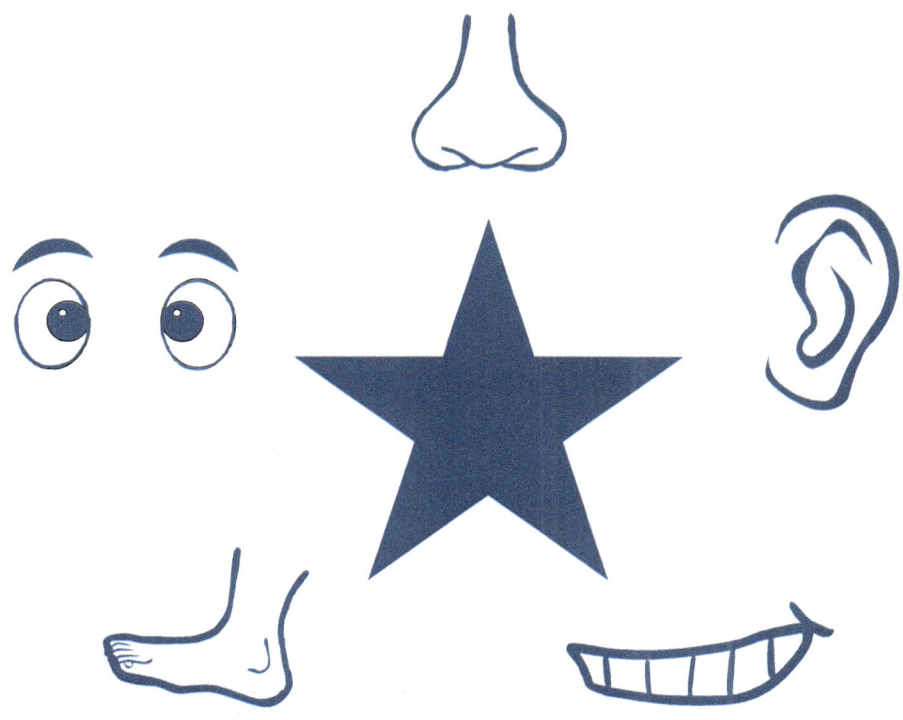

This is a parallelogram.

But on Father's Day, this shape is called *destruction*.

That parallelogram
used to look like this.
But a kid got to it.
You can guess what happened.

This is a heart.

But on Father's Day, this shape is called *unconditional*.

A father's love is so big, you can't measure it. It started growing as soon as he became a dad and there's nothing like it.
Except maybe the unconditional love his kids feel towards him. Even if they don't laugh at all of his jokes.

www.ingramcontent.com/pod-product-compliance
Lightning Source LLC
Chambersburg PA
CBHW061402010526
44119CB00010B/238